Mike and Spike

by Tristan Horrom
illustrated by Kate Flanagan

Decodable 15

McGraw Hill Education

Bothell, WA • Chicago, IL • Columbus, OH • New York, NY

MHEonline.com

Send all inquiries to:
McGraw-Hill Education
8787 Orion Place
Columbus, OH 43240

ISBN: 978-0-02-145182-1
MHID: 0-02-145182-6

Printed in China

9 10 11 12 13 DSS 28 27 26 25 24

Mike did not have a pup.

Mike is five!

Mike gets Spike!

Mike and Spike hike up and down.

They like to hike and have fun.

They like to ride a bike.

Spike is big!
Down, Spike, down!